W9-AQS-898

WITHDRAWN

3/16   2x   LC 12/15

RIVER FOREST PUBLIC LIBRARY
735 Lathrop Avenue
River Forest, Illinois 60305
708 / 366-5205

6/15

THE BEST JOB EVER

Movie Star

Ian F. Mahaney

PowerKiDS press.

New York

Published in 2015 by The Rosen Publishing Group, Inc.
29 East 21st Street, New York, NY 10010

Copyright © 2015 by The Rosen Publishing Group, Inc.

All rights reserved. No part of this book may be reproduced in any form without permission in writing from the publisher, except by a reviewer.

First Edition

Editor: Caitie McAneney
Book Design: Katelyn Heinle

Photo Credits: Cover, pp. 3–24 (background design) Toria/Shutterstock.com; cover (boy) Adam Taylor/Digital Vision/Getty Images; p. 5 Jaguar PS/Shutterstock.com; p. 7 (top) Handout/Getty Images News/Getty Images; p. 7 (bottom) Asianet-Pakistan/ Shutterstock.com; p. 8 cinemafestival/Shutterstock.com; pp. 9, 13 Featureflash/ Shutterstock.com; p. 10 Hill Street Studios/Blend Images/Getty Images; p. 11 Everett Collection/Shutterstock.com; p. 14 TORSTEN BLACKWOOD/AFP/ Getty Images; pp. 15 (Johnny Depp), 20 DFree/Shutterstock.com; p. 15 (Anna Kendrick) Helga Esteb/Shutterstock.com; p. 17 Kenneth Man/Shutterstock.com; p. 18 Rommel Canlas/Shutterstock.com; p. 19 Anton Oparin/Shutterstock.com; p. 21 (bottom) James Devaney/WireImage/Getty Images; p. 21 (top) Terence Walsh/ Shutterstock.com; p. 22 Gary Gershoff/WireImage/Getty Images.

Library of Congress Cataloging-in-Publication Data

Mahaney, Ian F.
Movie star / by Ian F. Mahaney.
p. cm. — (The best job ever)
Includes index.
ISBN 978-1-4994-0116-5 (pbk.)
ISBN 978-1-4994-0077-9 (6-pack)
ISBN 978-1-4994-0101-1 (library binding)
1. Motion picture acting — Vocational guidance — Juvenile literature. I. Mahaney, Ian F. II. Title.
PN1995.9.A26 M34 2015
791.4302—d23

Manufactured in the United States of America

CPSIA Compliance Information: Batch #CW15PK: For Further Information contact Rosen Publishing, New York, New York at 1-800-237-9932

Contents

BEING A MOVIE STAR

Think of your favorite movies. Do you know that it usually takes hundreds of people to make a movie? Some of these people are actors, and the ones in the starring **roles** are movie stars.

An actor's job is to understand the character they're trying to play. Then, the actor works to make the **audience** believe they are that character. Some famous movie stars include Leonardo DiCaprio and Jennifer Lawrence. These are the people you see walking on the red carpet at an award show or when a movie comes out. What a life!

Life as a movie star seems too good to be true! Movie stars are invited to many events with other famous people. People love to take their picture.

Jennifer Lawrence

HARD WORK PAYS OFF

There are many different kinds of acting jobs. Some actors work on stage in plays and musicals, while others work in movies or on television. To be an actor, you have to work very hard for many long hours. Many actors think the hard work is worth it because they get to be creative every day.

A few lucky actors get to be movie stars. There are a lot of benefits. Movie stars earn a lot of money doing what they love. They also get to meet many important people. Another benefit of being a movie star is being able to **influence** people all over the world.

Angelina Jolie is a movie star who influences people to give to charity. She supports causes that help those who are poor, need medical help, or are **refugees**.

ACTING SCHOOL

Many movie stars study acting for years before they land a big role. Some learn from **experience**, by acting in community theater and school plays. Other people go to school for acting. Many **colleges** offer theater **programs** that teach students acting skills, such as speaking clearly and getting into character. College theater programs usually last two to four years. Many schools and groups offer summer programs for people who can't go to school all year.

Some actors don't believe in learning acting in school. They feel acting school teaches skills that students can learn and practice on their own.

MOVIE STAR BIO: MERYL STREEP

Meryl Streep studied acting at Yale University. She has acted in many movies since the 1970s, including *Out of Africa* and *Mamma Mia!* She's considered one of the best actresses around.

Denzel Washington earned his bachelor's degree in theater from Fordham University. Today, he's one of the top movie stars in Hollywood!

HIGH SCHOOL PLAYS

High school students can begin acting even before they decide to study acting in college. Most high schools offer theater **productions** every year that give young people a chance to learn and practice acting skills. Katie Holmes is a movie star who began her career by acting in high school musicals.

Movie star Ashton Kutcher got his start by acting in high school plays.

After high school, actors can also practice acting in college theater or community theater. These productions are great opportunities for amateur (AA-muh-chur), or beginning, actors to practice acting. Acting in community productions is also a good way to land bigger roles. You never know who might be in the audience!

DIFFERENT ROLES

Movie stars usually have the leading roles in movies. Leading roles are the most important characters. Actors who play leading roles are usually shown on posters or in **trailers** for the movie.

Actors need to prove themselves in smaller roles before someone will hire them for leading roles. Actors known as extras have very small roles. Extras often appear in movies as part of a crowd. With that experience, someone may hire an actor for a small speaking part. They might get to say a line or two! The roles just below the leading roles are sometimes called supporting roles.

It can take years for actors to advance to supporting roles and even longer to advance to leading roles.

Leonardo DiCaprio and Hilary Swank

Many movie stars get their start in acting roles that aren't on the movie screen. Some find jobs acting in **commercials**. Other actors find jobs acting in TV shows.

Some actors **perform** in plays and musicals held in theaters. Acting in a theater is called stage acting. It's different from acting in a movie because actors perform before a live audience. Also, the show is performed over and over for different audiences, and each performance can be a little different. Some actors like stage acting better than movie acting because they feel closer to their audience. Others decide to leave the stage for the big screen!

MOVIE STAR BIO: JOHNNY DEPP

As a young actor, Johnny Depp acted in the television show *21 Jump Street*. He became a movie star well-known for his colorful, creative characters. He starred in *Pirates of the Caribbean* and *Charlie and the Chocolate Factory*.

Broadway is a famous area of New York City where major theaters are located. Movie star Anna Kendrick started acting in a Broadway musical when she was 12 years old.

AUDITIONS

When a movie company needs actors, they have auditions. During an audition, actors read the parts of different characters. Sometimes an actor reads alone. This one-sided performance is called a monologue. Other times, the company asks the actors to read a side. A side is a **script** with two parts that actors read aloud together.

Movie companies want to hear many actors read the script. After many actors audition, the company decides which actors are best for the parts. To prepare for an audition, actors should get to know the character they're trying to be.

Before an audition, actors should know how old the character is, where they're from, and what they're like. The actor should practice speaking as the character would speak.

FINDING FAME

Often the companies that hire actors put the word out in newspapers and magazines or on websites. Usually, only agents know about higher-paying jobs. An agent is a person who finds jobs for actors. In return for helping an actor find a job, the actor pays the agent a small portion of the money the actor earns on that job.

Finding an agent can be hard. Actors need to prove their talent and experience to the agent. The actor usually sends the agent a picture called a headshot. They can also send a résumé (REH-zuh-may), or list of experiences, roles, and skills.

You need a résumé for almost any job you want. On acting résumés, actors list the plays, commercials, TV shows, or movies they've been in, as well as their education.

ON THE SET

Remember how hundreds of people work together to make a movie? That means there are many ways to work in show business aside from acting. The screenwriter writes the movie. Some people work the cameras and lights, and others **design** the sets. Other people choose music to match the scenes. After filming is over, some people edit the movie by putting different scenes together.

A film's director has one of the most important jobs on a movie set. The director takes a script and makes it into a movie. They direct the actors and make sure the final film is ready for the big screen!

MOVIE STAR BIO: BEN AFFLECK

Ben Affleck is a movie star who decided to become a director. Affleck rose to fame in the 1990s, starring in movies such as *Armageddon* and *Good Will Hunting*. He began directing movies in 2007.

The people who act in a movie are called the cast.
The people who are behind the scenes are called the crew.

BREAK A LEG!

Acting in a movie can be a dream come true! Many actors think their job is fun and exciting. Acting gives people the opportunity to be creative every day. It takes a lot of time, talent, and luck to become a movie star.

If you want to try to be a movie star, you can start right away. You can take acting classes and audition for commercials. You can read scripts and practice playing a character. You can even find community or school plays to act in. Most of all, never give up a chance for acting experience. Break a leg! That's what actors say to mean "Good luck!"

Glossary

audience: A group of people gathered to see or hear something.

college: A school after high school.

commercial: A TV or radio message trying to sell something.

design: To plan the way something will look.

experience: Knowledge or skill gained by doing or seeing something.

influence: Having the power to sway others.

perform: To sing, dance, act, or play an instrument in front of other people.

production: A show.

program: A course of study.

refugee: A person who leaves his or her own country to find safety.

role: A part played by a person in a movie, TV show, or play.

script: The written story of a play, movie, or radio or television program.

trailer: A commercial for a movie that shows clips from the movie.

Index

A
Affleck, Ben, 20
agents, 18
audition, 16, 22

B
Broadway, 15

C
cast, 21
character, 4, 8, 12, 15, 16, 22
colleges, 8, 10, 11
commercials, 14, 19, 22
community theater, 8, 11, 22
crew, 21

D
Depp, Johnny, 15
director, 20

E
experience, 8, 12, 18, 22
extras, 12

H
high school, 10, 11

L
leading roles, 12

M
musicals, 6, 10, 14, 15

P
plays, 6, 8, 11, 14, 19, 22

R
résumé, 18, 19

S
screenwriter, 20
stage, 6, 14
Streep, Meryl, 8
supporting roles, 10

T
television, 6, 14, 15, 19

Websites

Due to the changing nature of Internet links, PowerKids Press has developed an online list of websites related to the subject of this book. This site is updated regularly. Please use this link to access the list: www.powerkidslinks.com/bje/movi

24